It's a Baby
Raccoon!

Kelly Doudna

Consulting Editor, Diane Craig, M.A./Reading Specialist

ABDO
Publishing Company

Published by ABDO Publishing Company, 8000 West 78th Street, Edina, Minnesota 55439.

Printed in the United States.

Editor: Pam Price
Content Developer: Nancy Tuminelly
Cover and Interior Design and Production: Mighty Media
Photo Credits: Design Pics Inc., Digital Vision, Peter Arnold Inc. (BIOS Klein & Hubert, H. Reinhard, P. Wegner, L. Weyers), Photodisc, ShutterStock

Library of Congress Cataloging-in-Publication Data

Doudna, Kelly, 1963-
    It's a baby raccoon! / Kelly Doudna.
        p. cm. -- (Baby mammals)
    ISBN 978-1-60453-030-8
    1. Raccoon--Infancy--Juvenile literature. I. Title.

    QL737.C26D68 2008
    599.76'32139--dc22

                        2007033745

SandCastle™ Level: Fluent

SandCastle™ books are created by a team of professional educators, reading specialists, and content developers around five essential components—phonemic awareness, phonics, vocabulary, text comprehension, and fluency—to assist young readers as they develop reading skills and strategies and increase their general knowledge. All books are written, reviewed, and leveled for guided reading, early reading intervention, and Accelerated Reader® programs for use in shared, guided, and independent reading and writing activities to support a balanced approach to literacy instruction. The SandCastle™ series has four levels that correspond to early literacy development. The levels are provided to help teachers and parents select appropriate books for young readers.

Emerging Readers	Beginning Readers	Transitional Readers	Fluent Readers
(no flags)	(1 flag)	(2 flags)	(3 flags)

SandCastle™ would like to hear from you. Please send us your comments and suggestions.
sandcastle@abdopublishing.com

Vital Statistics

for the Raccoon

BABY NAME
cub

NUMBER IN LITTER
1 to 7, average 4

WEIGHT AT BIRTH
2 to 3 ounces

AGE OF INDEPENDENCE
6 to 12 months

ADULT WEIGHT
5 to 30 pounds

LIFE EXPECTANCY
about 3 years

A mother raccoon makes her den in a hollow tree. Her cubs are born blind and helpless.

In about 10 days, a cub's black mask becomes visible.

Raccoon cubs stay in their tree dens for the first two months.

A mother raccoon raises her cubs without help from the father.

When cubs are two months old, they start learning how to climb, swim, and hunt.

Raccoons are good climbers. Cubs are comfortable playing in trees.

A raccoon can survive a fall from 35 or 40 feet high without being hurt.

Human activities cause the most raccoon deaths. Raccoons are hunted in many areas. They also die in traffic accidents.

Raccoons avoid wild predators by staying in their dens during the day.

Raccoons are omnivores. They will eat anything, from fish and berries to pet food and garbage.

Raccoons use their front paws like hands. They snatch fish out of water. They grab mice and insects out of holes.

Most raccoon cubs leave their mothers by the time they are one year old.

Fun Fact

About the Raccoon

There are up to 20 times more raccoons per square mile living in urban and suburban areas than in rural areas.

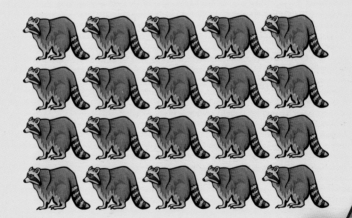

Glossary

accident – an unplanned event, often causing harm or damage.

avoid – to stay away from.

den – a small hollow used by an animal for shelter.

expectancy – an expected or likely amount.

hollow – having an empty space inside.

independence – the state of no longer needing others to care for or support you.

omnivore – one who eats both meat and plants.

predator – an animal that hunts others.

rural – of or related to the countryside.

urban – of or related to a city.

visible – able to be seen.

To see a complete list of SandCastle™ books and other nonfiction titles from ABDO Publishing Company, visit **www.abdopublishing.com**.

8000 West 78th Street, Edina, MN 55439

800-800-1312 • 952-831-1632 fax